About This Series

The *First Words* series provides emerging readers with multiple opportunities to practice reading high-frequency words used in simple text. These books are appropriate for independent, shared, and guided reading.

Red Rebus Section (pages 4–11) Each spread features a predictable, repetitive rebus sentence with a familiar picture clue placed opposite a full-page photograph that strongly supports the text.

Blue Story Section (pages 12–17) An illustrated short story containing the featured sight words offers contextual, repetitive reading opportunities using simple text and familiar letter-sound correspondence.

Green Game Section (pages 18–21) A fun, read-together guessing game based upon the contents of the book expands vocabulary and increases comprehension.

Rebus Glossary (page 22) This list pairs the words and picture clues featured in the rebus sentences.

SandCastle First Thirty Sight Words List (page 23) Use this list to build phonics and word recognition strategies for emerging and beginning readers.

Sight Word Focus

a   here   is

Here is a .

Here is a .

Here is a .

Here is a .

Here Is a Zoo

Here is a tiger.

Here is a panda.

Here is a zoo.

Look at me!

I have fur.

I have stripes.

I can roar.

What am I?

I am a tiger!

Rebus Glossary

monkey

panda

tiger

zebra

SandCastle
First Thirty Sight Words

a	here	not
am	I	on
and	in	said
are	is	see
at	it	the
big	like	this
can	little	to
come	look	up
for	me	we
go	my	you

About SandCastle™

A professional team of educators, reading specialists, and content developers created the SandCastle™ series to support young readers as they develop reading skills and strategies and increase their general knowledge. The SandCastle™ series has four levels that correspond to early literacy development in young children. The levels are provided to help teachers and parents select the appropriate books for young readers.

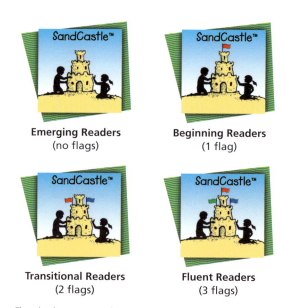

Emerging Readers
(no flags)

Beginning Readers
(1 flag)

Transitional Readers
(2 flags)

Fluent Readers
(3 flags)

These levels are meant only as a guide. All levels are subject to change.

To see a complete list of SandCastle™ books and other nonfiction titles from ABDO Publishing Company, visit **www.abdopub.com** or contact us at:
4940 Viking Drive, Edina, Minnesota 55435 • 1-800-800-1312 • fax: 1-952-831-1632